SPITFIRE
— A Living Legend —

D140197I

Osprey Colour Series

SPITFIRE
— A Living Legend —

JEREMY FLACK

T2819 Spitfire 10/11 pt Ehr 19 em Galley 1

Published in 1985 by Osprey Publishing Limited
12–14 Long Acre, London WC2E 9LP
Member company of the George Philip Group

© Jeremy Flack 1985

This book is copyrighted under the Berne Convention. All
rights reserved. Apart from any fair dealing for the purpose
of private study, research, criticism or review, as permitted
under the Copyright Act, 1956, no part of this publication
may be reproduced, stored in a retrieval system, or
transmitted in any form or by any means, electronic,
electrical, chemical, mechanical, optical, photocopying,
recording or otherwise, without prior written permission. All
enquiries should be addressed to the Publishers.

British Library Cataloguing in Publication Data

Flack, Jeremy
    Spitfire: a living legend.—(Osprey colour
    series)
    1. Spitfire (Fighter planes)
    I. Title
    623.74'64   UG1242.F5

    ISBN 0-85045-619-3

Editor Dennis Baldry
Designed by David Tarbutt
Printed in Italy

Front cover Spitfire LF Mk Vc AR501 owned by the
Shuttleworth Collection, flown on this occasion by
Angus McVittie

Title page The Battle of Britain Memorial Flight's
Spitfire Mk II, P7350, taxies out

Back cover Spitfire sunset: G-FIRE is a Mk XIV
operated by Classic Air Displays from Elstree

Contents

Jeremy Flack is the company photographer of Square D, a Swindon-based company which produces electrical switch gear for a wide variety of industrial applications. But during his spare time, he is better known to aviation enthusiasts for his photographic exploits on behalf of Aviation Photographs International (API). Launched in 1969 and jointly run by his wife, Julie, API is well established as a reliable and efficient source of civil and military aircraft transparencies.

The vast majority of the material in *SPITFIRE: A LIVING LEGEND* was shot in Southern England between March 1984 and February 1985 using Minolta cameras and lenses, loaded with Fuji 50, Kodachrome 25 and 64. A Cessna 182, Cessna Hawk XP, Piper Seneca I, T-6, and a P-40E Kittyhawk were used for the air-to-air sequences.

To my wife, Julie.

This book is not a history of the Spitfire (one day, somebody will write it) but a photographic portfolio set in a modern, high technology age. Today, we tend to look at the Spitfire as a quintessential work of aerodynamic art in its own right, rather than as an aeroplane designed to destroy enemy aircraft as efficiently as possible. Its name, beauty, and track record has made it pre-eminent among Allied wartime aircraft in the minds of the British public, pilots, and enthusiasts ever since it personified the spirit of national resistance against Nazi tyranny when Britain stood alone in the long, hot summer of 1940.

For Supermarine, the Spitfire marked both the apex and the end of their brief foray into the fighter business, for despite the efforts of chief designer Joe Smith and his talented team, the post-war Attacker, Swift, and Scimitar were at best undistinguished, and at worst a complete disaster. Until the Sandys' Defence White Paper in 1957, Hawker effectively regained the driving seat in British fighter aviation.

When the 50th anniversary of the Battle of Britain is celebrated in 1990, there will be even more Spitfires in the air than today. Another generation will hear the sound of freedom and see one of the world's best loved aeroplanes.

Jeremy Flack
Swindon,
Wiltshire

Wing leader

Originally delivered as a Spitfire LF Mk IX (Merlin 66), MH434/G-ASJV is now powered by a Merlin 76, a right-hand tractor unit from a de Havilland Mosquito. The engine has a maximum continuous rating of 1375 hp (2850 rpm + 12 lb of boost) at an altitude of 13,500 ft, consuming 100L avgas at the rate of 150 gallons per hour.

MH434 was one of 5095 Mk IXs built at the Castle Bromwich Aircraft Factory (CBAF) and it entered service with No 222 (Natal) Sqn in 1943. During its career with this unit the aircraft was credited with two Fw 190s destroyed, and a shared kill on a Bf 109F. It

saw further action after WW II with the Royal Netherlands Air Force in Indonesia. Today, MH434 wears No 222 Sqn codes again and the machine is operated by The Old Flying Machine Company from Duxford Airfield. **Left** Mark Hanna nears the top of a loop. **Below** Holding formation on a P-51D Mustang when MH434 sported the initials of its former owner Adrian Swire. **Overleaf** Mark Hanna's father, Ray, is flying the Curtiss P-40E Kittyhawk owned by John Paul of Alamo, California. Codes 'SU-E' spell out the first name of Paul's wife

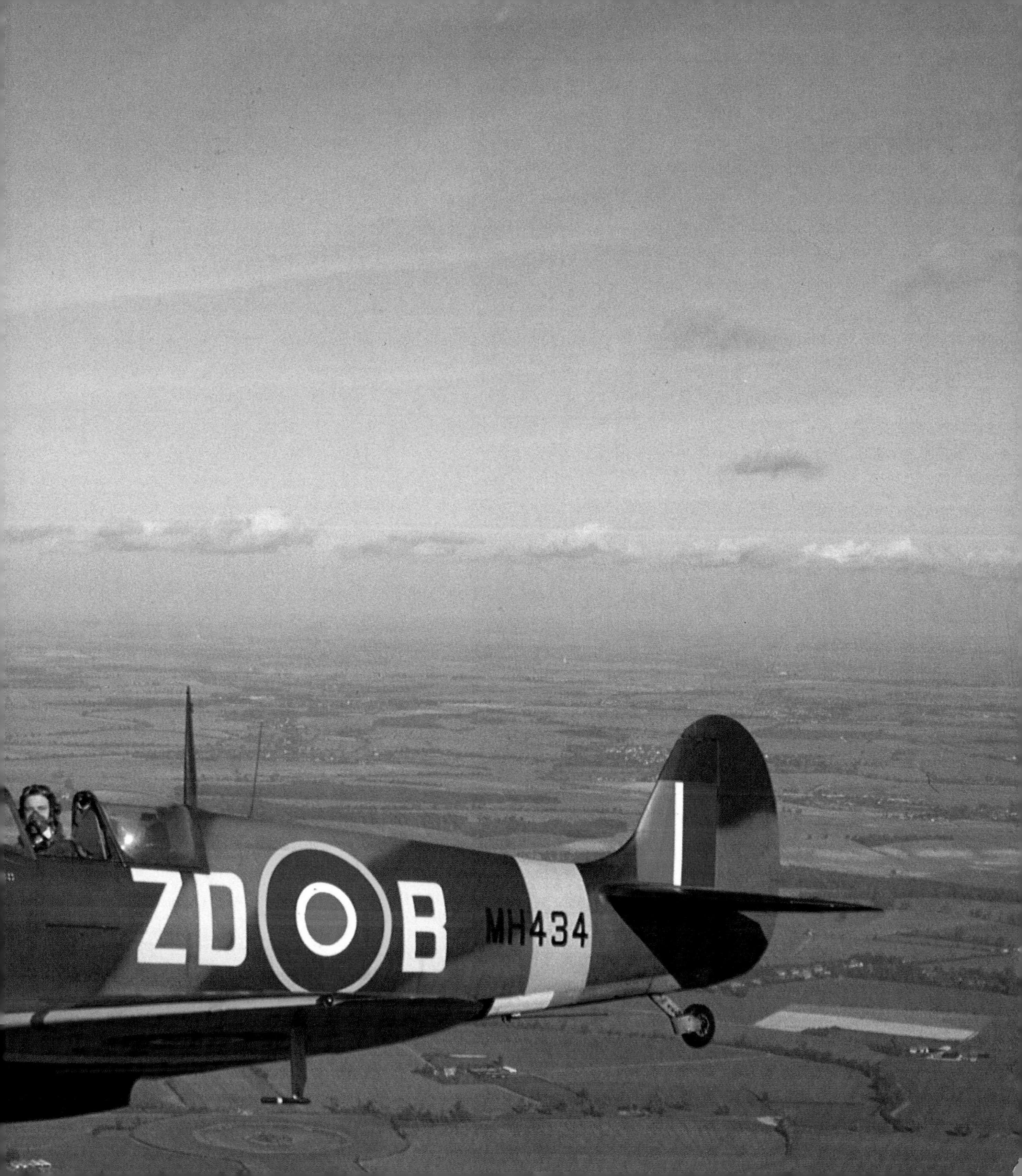
ZD B
MH434

Preceding pages and left Mark Hanna flying an
aerobatic sequence in MH434. A positive loading of 5G
must never be exceeded. **Below** Fast and low in the
Hanna tradition. **Overleaf** Making angels

Spitfire F Mk XIV owned by Rolls-Royce Ltd and based at Castle Donington near Derby. RM689/G-ALGT has accumulated only 1000 flying hours. Its Griffon 65 engine delivers 2050 hp at 2750 rpm and +12 lb of boost. Ex-Rolls-Royce chief test pilot Cliff Rogers is at the controls, poised yet relaxed below a Cessna 182. Purists will point out that despite being coded 'AP-D', this Spitfire never served with No 130 Sqn. But isn't the sight and sound of its airborne majesty more important? **Right and overleaf** G-FIRE has been transformed since it was re-discovered with its outer wings hacked off in a Belgian scrap yard and bought for £250. A variety of owners and £100,000 later (spent by Spencer Flack), Spitfire FR Mk XIVe (NH904) is now resplendent in striking scarlet. The restoration was handled by Mike Searle at Ambrion Aviation, Elstree. G-FIRE is now owned by the Classic Air Displays syndicate, also based at Elstree. For the last shot in the following sequence, pilot Ken Whitehead uses only a whisker of power from G-FIRE's 2050 horse Griffon 65 to 'loose deuce' with Mike Searle's half-scale WAR Fw 190 replica adorned in II/JG 1 'Oesau' warpaint

Page 26/27 and inset Clipped-wing Spitfire LF Mk Vc (AR501/G-AWII) is owned by the Shuttleworth Collection. It was built by Westland Aircraft, issued to No 310 (Czech) Sqn in July 1942, and assigned to Sqn Ldr F. Dolezal, DFC. When the aircraft was flown by the late Neil Williams in 1975 after two years of painstaking restoration, it was authentically repainted in its original markings. At the time of writing, AR510 is grounded after severe corrosion was discovered in the root of a propeller blade. Clipping the wing improved its geometric efficiency, increasing speed and the rate of roll at low level to combat the Bf 109F. But the extra induced drag and loss of lift had a negative effect on landing and take-off run, range, and ceiling

Preceding page, this page, and overleaf Aldermaston is better known today for nuclear weapon research and the design and manufacture of nuclear warheads, but in 1945 Spitfire FR Mk XIV NH749 emerged from the Aldermaston works of Vickers-Armstrongs. After NH749 was despatched to Karachi, India, in July 1945, its history with the Indian Air Force is extremely difficult to decipher. However, the late Ormond Haydon-Baillie brought it back to England in 1978 where it was re-sold to A. and K. Wickenden and subsequently registered as G-MXIV on 11 April 1980. By 1983 the aircraft had been restored to flying condition by Keith Wickenden and it was offered for sale at Christie's aircraft auction at Duxford, but a final bid of £180,000 failed to attain the reserve price. Sadly, Keith Wickenden died in a flying accident and G-MXIV will probably be sold in the near future

This page and overleaf Frenchman Roland Fraissinet is the owner of this Spitfire PR Mk XI (PL983/G-PRXI) which was impeccably restored to airworthiness by Phillip Tillyard of Trent Aero Engineering, based at East Midlands Airport (Castle Donington.) The aircraft is painted in the PRU Blue scheme used by No 4 Sqn, 2nd Tactical Air Force (TAF).

Speed meant survival in the photo reconnaissance business, every precious knot of airspeed reducing the risk of interception by enemy fighters—a Merlin-70 powered PR Mk XI was capable of 422 mph at 27,000 ft. Different types of cameras and lenses were carried to suit the particular requirements of each mission; options included F.8 cameras (20 inch focal length), F.24s (14 inch focal length), and F.52s (36 inch focal length.) Obliquely-mounted cameras in blister fairings could also be fitted outboard of each wheel well under the wing.

G-PRXI normally lives at Castle Donington and is expected to participate in a number of air shows across Western Europe. During a sojourn in France at the end of 1984, the aircraft was flown from Istres by no less a pilot than Mirage master Jean Marie Saget. The jockey on this occasion is Mike Searle

Preceding page 'Missing man' formation of Spitfires over the International Air Tattoo at Greenham Common in 1983 paid tribute to the memory of Sir Douglas Bader, the famous WW II fighter ace. **Above and right** Spitfire LF Mk IXe (ML417) owned by Stephen Grey departs from Kemble where the paint job was completed. **Overleaf** Spitfire Mk II (P7350) of the Battle of Britain Memorial Flight over the hedge on finals to land. It has since been re-coded 'SH-D'

Spits in pieces: restoring a legend

The restoration and servicing of old aeroplanes is a difficult, time-consuming process, but Booker-based Personal Plane Services are more than equal to the task. Edna and Tony Bianchi are the power behind the company, formed in 1947 by the late Doug Bianchi and now busier than ever. **Left and bottom right** Stephen Grey's LF Mk IXe (ML417/G-BJSG) in primer is a born again single-seat Spitfire. Re-converting the aircraft from a T Mk 9 trainer involved re-siting the front cockpit 13 inches aft and many of the frames had to be built from scratch; areas of fuselage, wings, and tail were re-skinned. **Top right** Packed PPS hangar includes a fully painted ML417, a French-built Morane MS.500 (Fieseler Storch), and Kermit Weeks' Mosquito

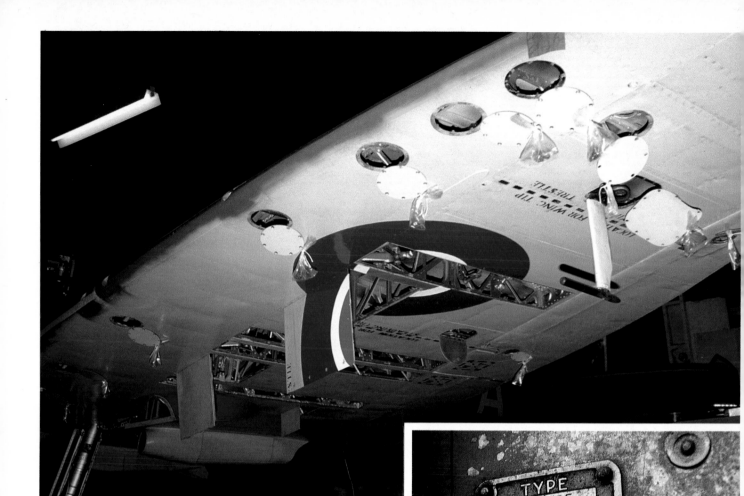

No shortage of access panels on the wing of Spitfire
Mk Ia AR213. **Inset** Mod plate of Spitfire LF Mk IXe
TE517 reveals that this was the 558th Mk IX built by
the Castle Bromwich Aircraft Factory (CBAF.) **Top
right** Engine bearer struts of Mk Ia AR213. **Below**
When its engine was pulled the c/n plate of the Heston
Aircraft Company emerged from behind a coat of paint

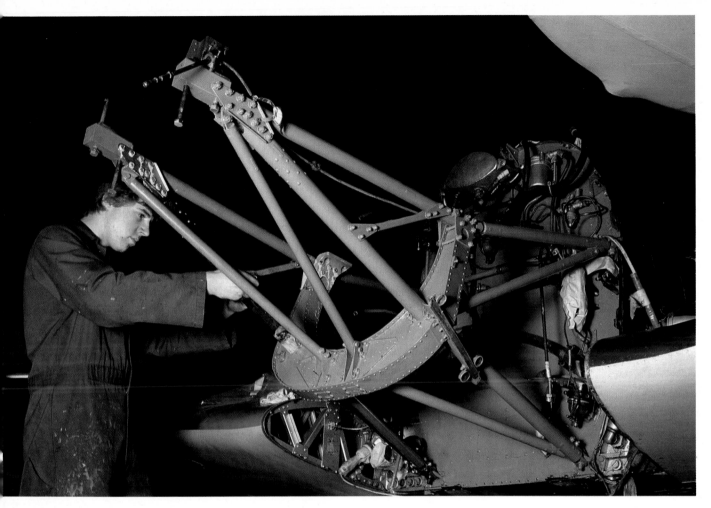

Spitfire LF Mk IX (TE517/G-BIXP) will be rebuilt to flying condition under the guidance of Dick Melton at Vintage Airworks, St Leonards-on-Sea. **Opposite page** The fuselage interior is grubby but the frames are in a satisfactory state. TE517 was sold to Israel in 1949 after serving in the advanced training role with the Czech Air Force. It was eventually recovered from a kibbutz near Gaaton in 1977. **Right** The wings are being restored by Trent Aero Engineering. **Above right** Connecting the hydraulics of the retractable tailwheel fitted to PR Mk XI PL983

49

Spitfire LF Mk IXe (TE566/G-BLCK) owned by
Steve Atkins at Vintage Airworks swops old skin for
new metal. **Right** Spitfire Mk IX (MJ730/G-BLAS)
nearing completion. **Opposite and overleaf** Spitfire
PR Mk XI PL983 being re-assembled by Trent Aero
Engineering in Rolls-Royce's hangar at East Midlands
Airport. Mk XIV RM689 in the foreground (overleaf)

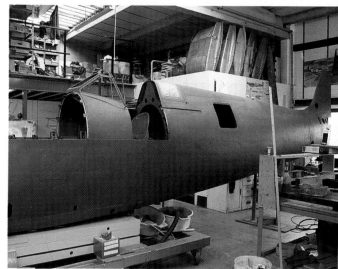

Structurally complete, the exterior of Spitfire PR Mk XI PL983 is carefully prepared and primed to obtain a high standard of finish. Inaccessible areas are sprayed before final assembly. **Above** The elevators and hinge control are presented to the fin and tailplane

Spray gunner gives a coat of PRU Blue to PL983.
Right The spinner and backplate are blue, too

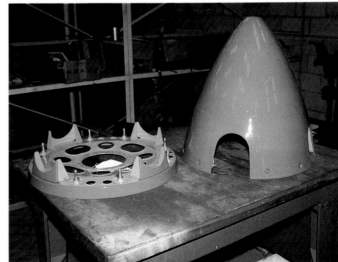

Spitfire LF Mk IXe ML417 being refuelled before a test flight. **Left** Internal and external attention. **Overleaf, left** Biggles' flies undone? Tony Bianchi confers with his team after an engine run. **Overleaf, right** The cockpit comes with all mod comms

ML417's Packard Merlin 266 running cleanly before and after the camouflage and markings were applied. The codes belong to No 443 (RCAF) Sqn, 2nd TAF, circa June 1944

Preceding page Immac Spitfire PR Mk XI PL983 taxies out for take-off at Castle Donington in the summer of '84. Inset Its Packard Merlin 266 was purchased from Jack Hovey and shipped from the States. Phillip Tillyard (right) keeps a watchful eye on the engine as it fires up in the airframe for the first time. Above Turnin' and burnin' at Duxford. Right Extra ballast is required to hold the tail down with the throttle wide open

A Spitfire built for two

During WW II the demand for Spitfire fighters was enormous (more than 20,000 were built in two dozen major marks) and no production capacity was allocated to two-seat trainer versions. After the war about 20 airframes were bastardized from existing Mk IXs and exported to a small number of air forces. T Mk 9 ML407/G-LFIX (below) started life at Castle Bromwich as an LF Mk IXc and saw operational service with No 485 (RNZAF) Sqn from April 1944 until January 1945. After conversion by Vickers, ML407 was sold to the Irish Air Corps in 1951 and operated from Baldonnel as IAC162 until its retirement in 1960. Nick Grace acquired the aircraft in 1979 and has completed a five year restoration at St Merryn, Cornwall, for the British Aviation Heritage

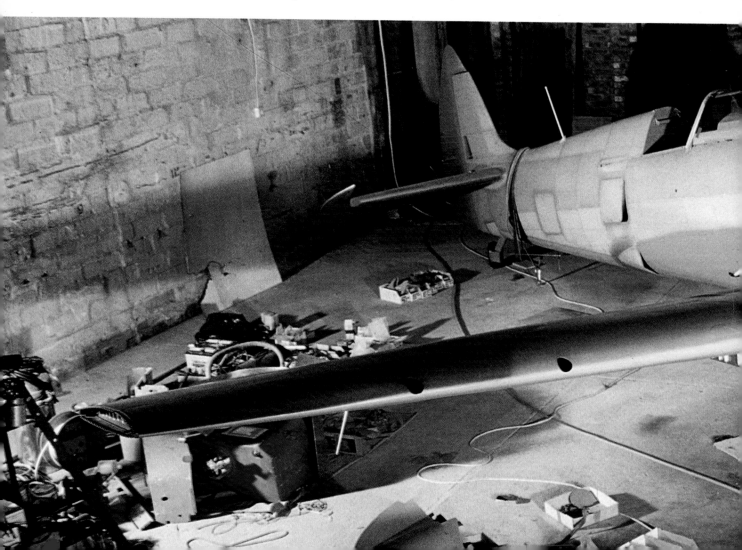

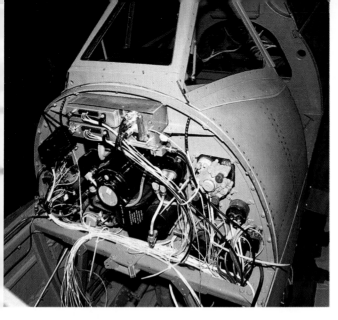

Left Fitting and wiring the instruments in the front cockpit prior to installing the main upper fuel tank. **Overleaf** The front (left) and rear cockpits of G-LFIX. Large spade grip on the stick was hinged for lateral control, while the whole column moved fore and aft for pitch imputs

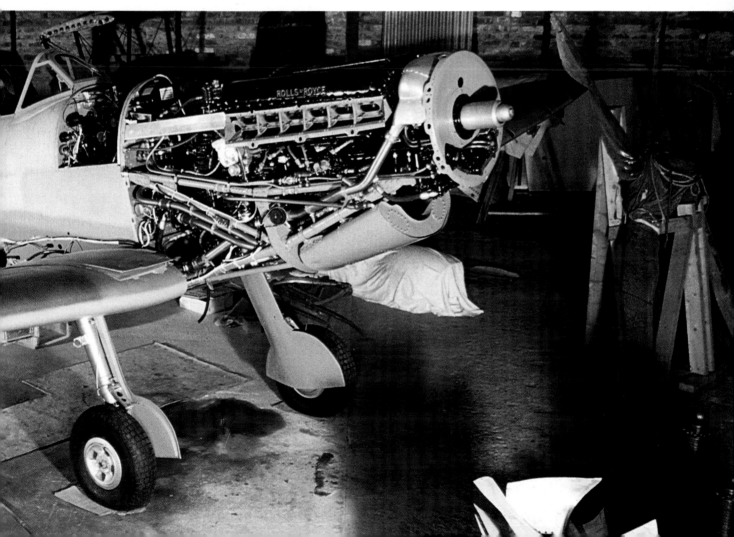

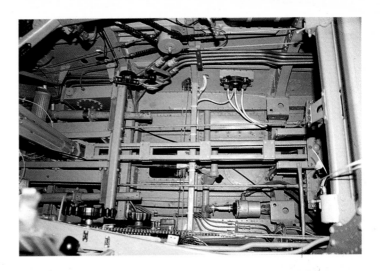

Left Two-seat configuration looks strange. Fuel lines, control wires, and electrics are installed underneath the wing root fillet, or (right) along the bottom of fuselage under the pilots' seat. **Below** The Merlin 25 fitted to G-LFIX. **Overleaf** 'Spitfires do taxi in IMC'. In fact the smoke screen is the result of 30 years of inhibitor being blasted out of the Merlin's 12 cylinders. **Inset** Nick Grace and his wife, Carolyn, see clearly now the engine is running sweetly. **Page 74/75** G-AIDN in a variety of colour schemes. After a landing mishap at Coventry in 1978, the aircraft has remained in storage

Battle of Britain Memorial Flight

The BBMF was formed at Biggin Hill on 11 July 1957 to commemorate the major battle honour of the Royal Air Force, won against the *Luftwaffe* in the summer of 1940. **Below** Spitfire Mk II P7350 has served with the flight since October 1968. 'SH-D' (No 64 Sqn codes) is powered by a Merlin 35. **Right** Spitfire LF Mk Vb AB910 suffered appalling damage in August 1978

during an air show at Bex, Switzerland, when a Harvard chewed into it on the ground after swinging on take-off. After incredible repair work at Abingdon, the aircraft was returned to the flight, fully serviceable, on 26 October 1981. Strengthening plates on the wing (below right) are a visible legacy of the collision

Left, inset, and overleaf Spitfire PR Mk XIX PM631 is one of the original members of the BBMF. As part of the RAF's contribution to the 40th anniversary of D-Day, the aircraft was repainted in full invasion stripery as 'DL-E' of No 91 Sqn, circa June 1944. Interestingly, at the time of the Indonesian Confrontation in 1964, PM631 took part in dogfighting exercises with the supersonic English Electric Lightning interceptor, just in case the RAF was forced to mix it with Indonesian Air Force P-51 Mustangs—a somewhat extreme example of dissimilar air combat training

Preceding page Not a rare colour photograph of a wartime MU (maintenance unit), but the interior of the BBMF hangar at Coningsby, Lincolnshire, in December 1984. Four Spits, a Hurricane, and the world's only airworthy Lancaster bomber are being serviced. **Below** Spitfire LF Mk Vb AB910, this time in the earlier 'QJ-J' codes used by Jeffrey Quill. He flew during the Battle of Britain with No 92 Sqn during a 'break' from test flying the Spitfire. The aircraft is on jacks at No 5 MU at Kemble following a landing gear collapse at Duxford in June 1976—the damage was made good by 21 December. An Andover (perhaps better known in its civil guise as the 748) is in the background. **Right** Spitfire PR Mk XIX PS853 being modified to accept a Griffon 58 (ex-Shackleton.) A windfall of Griffon engines has been delayed by problems with the replacement for the Shackleton airborne early warning (AEW) aircraft, the BAe Nimrod AEW.3

Spitfires, Spit fliers

Mark (in cockpit) and Ray Hanna with Spitfire Mk IX MH434 consult each other before their display slots. **Below** Mark Hanna is normally an F-4 driver in the RAF, but looks equally at home in a Spitfire

Preceding page and above Spitfire spectacular at West Malling attracted Mk XIV G-FIRE, Mk XIV NH749/'L', Mk IX MH434/'ZD-B', Mk Ia AR213/'QG-A', LF Mk Vb AB910/'XT-M' and Hawker Hurricane Mk IIc PZ865 *The Last of the Many*, the final example built, sneaks in at the end. Hurricane production ceased in August 1944 at number 14,231, just as Spitfire output peaked at 500 per month. **Overleaf** Cherokee 140 serves to emphasize the beautifully proportioned lines of the Spitfire Mk XIV. NH749 is based at the Cranfield College of Aeronautics and students are happy to have their lectures interrupted when Angus McVittie (inset) takes her for a test flight

Preceding page The chocks are pulled away from
MH434 at North Weald. **Inset** Ray Hanna chatting to
engineer Roger Shepherd, the man responsible for
keeping the aircraft serviceable. **Left** The Honourable
Patrick Lindsay's Spitfire Mk Ia (AR213/G-AIST)
parked at Alconbury. **Below** Sitting pretty at North
Weald in 1984: the groundcrew relax on the grass
underneath MH434, recreating a timeless image
repeated at many Spitfire dispersals during WW II.
Overleaf Spitfire LF Mk IXc NH238 seems to have
got it a bit rich

103—

Preceding page with insets NH238/G-MKIX is one of the many Spitfires acquired by Doug Arnold of Warbirds of Great Britain. Presently based at Blackbushe, the aircraft is expected to move to Bitteswell with the rest of his warbird collection. G-MKIX was formerly resident in the States as N238V, painted to represent the Spitfire Mk IX 'JE-J' flown by wing leader Johnny Johnson, and used to score the majority of his 38 kills. **Top left** Wg Cdr 'Dicky' Martin in the cockpit of the Shuttleworth Collection's LF Mk Vc. **Bottom left** Spitfire Mk Vb BL614 has been one of the star attractions of the Manchester Air & Space Museum since 1982. Unlike the airworthy Mk Vs, BL614 is fitted with the correct exhaust stubs common to Merlin-engined Spitfires until the introduction of the Merlin 60 series in the marks VII, VIII, and IX with individual ejectors. The aircraft has been restored to No 222 (Natal) Sqn codes 'ZD-F' which it wore when the RAF provided air cover for the bloody Dieppe raid in August 1942. **Above** Mike Searle poses in PR Mk XI PL983

Spit bits

The Spitfire's long snout plus tail-dragger undercarriage equals practically zero forward visibility. Weaving is essential to avoid expensive noises up front when you are manoeuvring on the ground. This is a Merlin-powered Spitfire Mk IX (MH434). Staying with the subject of visibility, until the cut down rear fuselage and 360-degree vision canopy were introduced a rear view mirror helped to check six and spot the bad guy curving in behind you. **Below** To prevent moisture being sucked into the engine as it cools off, disposable plastic cups are stuffed up the exhaust manifold exit pipes

Left Dave Reader tops up the oil tank of MH434 with Aeroshell W120; its Merlin 76 drinks 34 pints an hour at maximum continuous power. **Above** 'Sir, is one bidding or just picking one's nose? *Thank you*'. Gavel in hand, Spitfire owner and pilot, The Honourable Patrick Lindsay, officiates at Christie's aircraft sale at Duxford Airfield in 1984. A final bid of a cool £320,000 failed to meet the reserve price set for Roland Fraissinet's PR Mk XI. In the background a de Havilland Tiger Moth and a Dragon Rapide look on. Any offers? **Overleaf** The trolley-acc is pulled away after injecting 12 volts AC into the starter motor circuit of Shuttleworth's LF Mk Vc at Old Warden. **Page 110/111** German Hoffmann prop gives G-FIRE pulling power

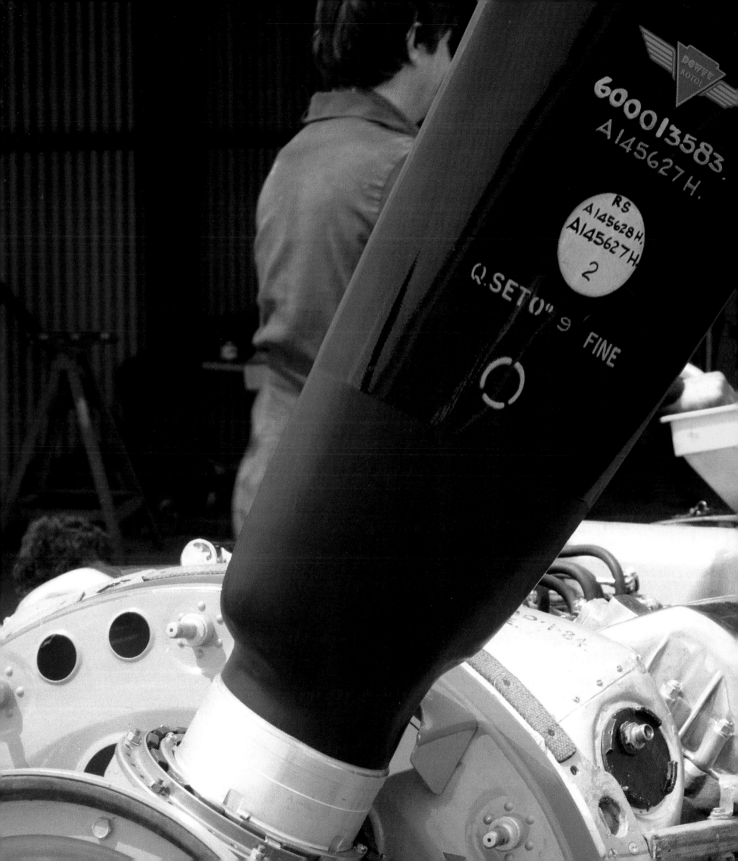

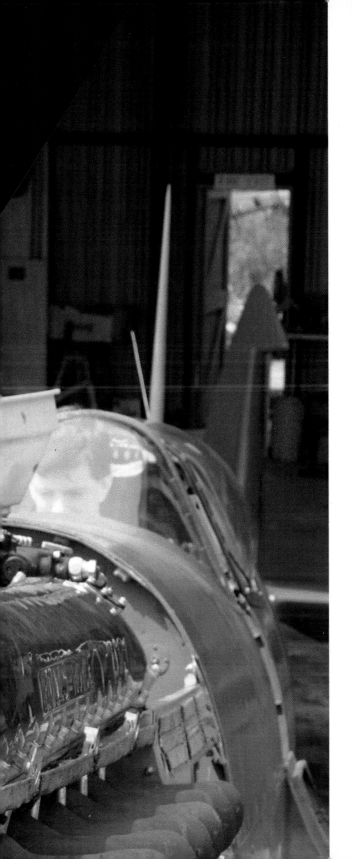

Left Zero-houred Dowty Rotol propeller fitted to PR Mk XI PL983 complete with logo. **Top** Oil-cooler intake of LF Mk Vc AR6501, mounted under the left wing. **Middle** Merlin production was augmented by Packard who built the engine under license in America. **Bottom** Carburettor air intake duct under the nose of LF Mk Vc AR501

Left Flashing strobe lights in the muzzles of G-FIRE's Hispanos are a big hit at air shows. **Bottom left** Gun camera port in the left wing root of LF Mk Vc AR501. **Bottom right** Wing strengthening and cannon fairing (introduced because of the size of the ammunition feed drum for the 20 mm Hispano) of LF Mk Vc AR501

This page, right and bottom right Hispano armament of LF Mk IXe ML417 indicates the provision for two additional cannons shown by the inboard stubs and space for a second fairing on the wing. If the two extra cannons were fitted, the four 0.303 Browning machine guns were deleted. **Below** Hispano installation on LF Mk Vc with cannon barrel fairing

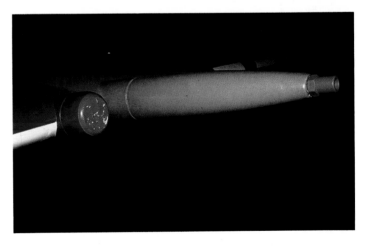

Spitting image? John Isaccs' 6/10ths scale Spitfire
replica G-BBJI is powered by a 100 hp Continental O-
200 flat-four engine giving a maximum speed of 150
mph. Fully aerobatic, its wooden airframe is stressed to
a healthy +9/4·5G; the landing gear is non-retractable.
Before he became a school master John Isaccs was
employed by Vickers at their Woolston works near
Southampton Water and was closely involved in
Spitfire production. G-BBJI first flew on 5 May 1975
and was originally painted silver overall, but PRU Blue
was the colour of the day at Duxford in 1984. **Right**
IFF (Identification Friend or Foe) was already in use
by the RAF at the beginning of WW II. Spitfire LF
Mk Vc AR501 is probably the only example with a pair
of authentic aerials. **Extreme right** Dr Gordon
Mitchell, the son of Spitfire designer R. J. Mitchell, in
front of Spitfire PR Mk XI PL983

Clive Du Cros is building this full-size flying replica of the prototype Spitfire K5054 in a secret location somewhere in Swindon. Nicknamed the 'wooden wonder', it is being constructed using douglas fir and sitka spruce covered by birch ply. Power will be provided by the specially modified Jaguar V12 automobile engine on the right. Du Cros aims to have the aeroplane ready for the 50th anniversary of the Spitfire's maiden flight, the historic event which took place at Eastleigh near Southampton when Capt J. 'Mutt' Summers, Vickers' chief test pilot, pulled back on the stick of K5054 on 5 March 1936. Unlike the original, the replica will probably have a tailwheel instead of a skid, the modified rudder with smaller horn balance, and fairings for the landing gear from the start. The *real* K5054 was written off after a landing accident at Farnborough on 4 September 1939

The normal and emergency landing gear ('chassis') operating controls. **Overleaf** Mark Hanna's leather flying helmet and mask ready for another air show scramble in MH434